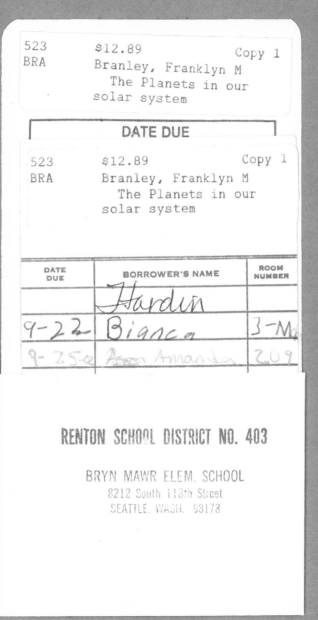

523	$12.89	Copy 1
BRA	Branley, Franklyn M	
	The Planets in our	
	solar system	

DATE DUE

523	$12.89	Copy 1
BRA	Branley, Franklyn M	
	The Planets in our	
	solar system	

DATE DUE	BORROWER'S NAME	ROOM NUMBER
	Hardin	
9-22	Bianca	3-M
9-25-0	Amanda	209

This Is a Let's-Read-and-Find-Out Science Book®

THE PLANETS IN OUR SOLAR SYSTEM

Revised Edition

Franklyn M. Branley

illustrated by

Don Madden

Thomas Y. Crowell   New York

Other Recent Let's-Read-and-Find-Out Science Books® You Will Enjoy

The Moon Seems to Change · Rockets and Satellites · Ant Cities · Get Ready for Robots!
Journey into a Black Hole · Gravity Is a Mystery · Snow Is Falling · Air Is All Around You
What the Moon Is Like · What Makes Day and Night · Turtle Talk · Hurricane Watch
Sunshine Makes the Seasons · My Visit to the Dinosaurs · The BASIC Book · Bits and Bytes
Germs Make Me Sick! · Flash, Crash, Rumble, and Roll · Volcanoes · Dinosaurs Are Different
What Happens to a Hamburger · Meet the Computer · How to Talk to Your Computer
Comets · Rock Collecting · Is There Life in Outer Space? · All Kinds of Feet
Flying Giants of Long Ago · Rain and Hail · Why I Cough, Sneeze, Shiver, Hiccup, and Yawn
You Can't Make a Move Without Your Muscles · The Sky Is Full of Stars
Digging Up Dinosaurs · No Measles, No Mumps for Me · When Birds Change Their Feathers
Birds Are Flying · A Jellyfish Is Not a Fish · Cactus in the Desert · Me and My Family Tree
Redwoods Are the Tallest Trees in the World · Shells Are Skeletons · Caves
Wild and Woolly Mammoths · The March of the Lemmings · Corals · Energy from the Sun
Corn Is Maize · The Eel's Strange Journey

The *Let's-Read-and-Find-Out Science Book* series was originated by Dr. Franklyn M. Branley, Astronomer Emeritus and former Chairman of the American Museum–Hayden Planetarium, and was formerly co-edited by him and Dr. Roma Gans, Professor Emeritus of Childhood Education, Teachers College, Columbia University. For a complete catalog of Let's-Read-and-Find-Out Science Books, write to Thomas Y. Crowell Junior Books, Harper & Row, Publishers, Inc., 10 East 53rd Street, New York, NY 10022.

Grateful acknowledgment is made to NASA/JPL for the photographs on pages 4 and 5; Mount Wilson and Las Campanas Observatories, Carnegie Institution of Washington for the photograph on page 10; NASA for the photograph of Comet West on page 13; and the Hansen Planetarium for the photograph of the meteoroid on page 13.

THE PLANETS IN OUR SOLAR SYSTEM
Text copyright © 1981 by Franklyn M. Branley
Illustrations copyright © 1981, 1987 by Don Madden
All rights reserved. No part of this book may be used or reproduced in any manner whatsoever without written permission except in the case of brief quotations embodied in critical articles and reviews. Printed in the United States of America. For information address Thomas Y. Crowell Junior Books, 10 East 53rd Street, New York, N.Y. 10022. Published simultaneously in Canada by Fitzhenry & Whiteside Limited, Toronto.
10 9 8 7 6 5 4 3 2 1
Revised Edition

Library of Congress Cataloging-in-Publication Data
Branley, Franklyn Mansfield, 1915–
    The planets in our solar system.
    (Let's-read-and-find-out science book)
    Summary: Introduces the solar system and its nine planets. Includes directions for making two models, one showing relative sizes of the planets and the other their relative distances from the sun.
    1. Planets—Juvenile literature. [1. Planets. 2. Solar system] I. Madden, Don, 1927–   ill.
II. Title. III. Series.
QB602.B73 1987   523.4   86-47530
ISBN 0-690-04579-4   ISBN 0-690-04581-6 (lib. bdg.)

We all live on a planet. Our planet is called Earth.
It is one of nine planets that go around the sun.

You probably know the names of some of the planets. Maybe you know all of them. The nine planets are Mercury, Venus, Earth, Mars, Jupiter, Saturn, Uranus, Neptune, and Pluto.

The nine planets are part of the solar system.

Surface of Mercury

These photographs show seven of the planets in our solar system. We don't yet have good close-up photographs of the others.

Venus

Jupiter

Earth

Saturn

Mars

Uranus

5

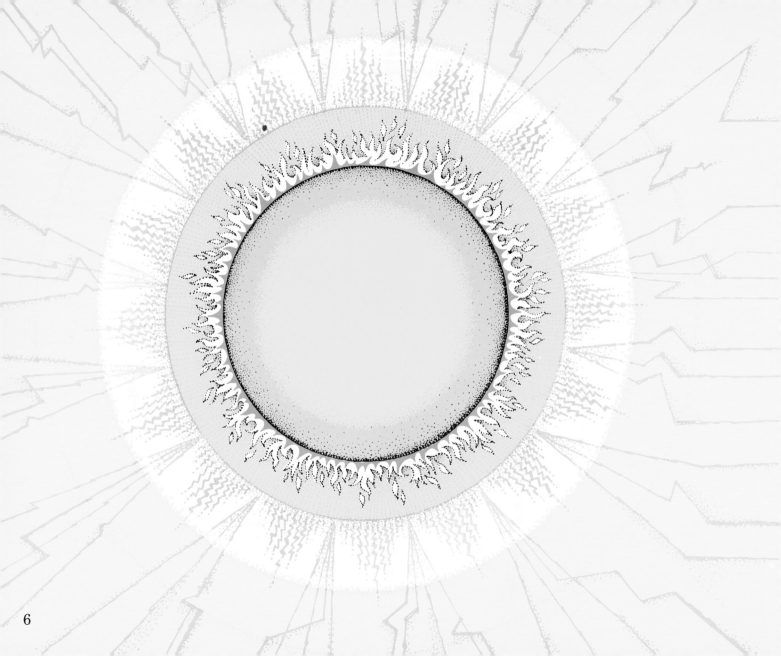

6

The most important part of the solar system is the sun. The word *sol* means sun. So, the solar system could be called the "sun system."

After the sun, the most important parts of the solar system are the nine planets.

Have you ever tried to find the planets in the sky? Uranus, Neptune, and Pluto are very dim. You need a telescope to see them.

You don't need a telescope to see Venus, Mars, Jupiter, or Saturn. They look like bright stars. You may have seen them and thought they were stars.

You don't need a telescope to see Mercury, either. You can see it in the early evening just after sunset or in the early morning just before sunrise. At these times, though, the sky is not very dark. You have to be a good sky watcher to find Mercury.

The moon

10

But there is another part of the solar system that you can easily see. It is the moon.

The moon goes around the Earth. It is sometimes called Earth's satellite.

Most of the other planets have satellites, too. But you need a telescope to see them.

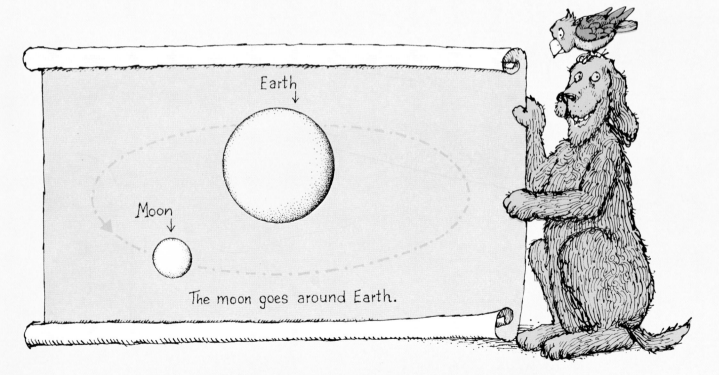

Earth

Moon

The moon goes around Earth.

Asteroids are also part of the solar system. So are comets and meteoroids. Asteroids are big chunks of rock that go around the sun. Many are as big as a house. Some are as big as a mountain, even bigger.

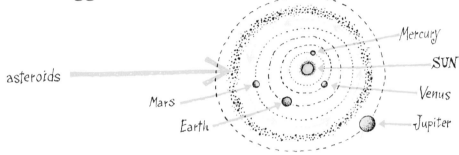

Comets are collections of ice, gas, and dust. The center of a comet may be only a few miles across, but the tail may be millions of miles long.

Meteoroids are bits of rock and metal. Some are large, but most are as small as grains of sand. Have you ever seen a shooting star? It was not really a star. It was a meteoroid falling toward Earth.

This is a photograph of a bright comet named Comet West, which is about 50 million miles long from head to tail.

The long streak in this photograph is the tail of a meteoroid falling toward Earth.

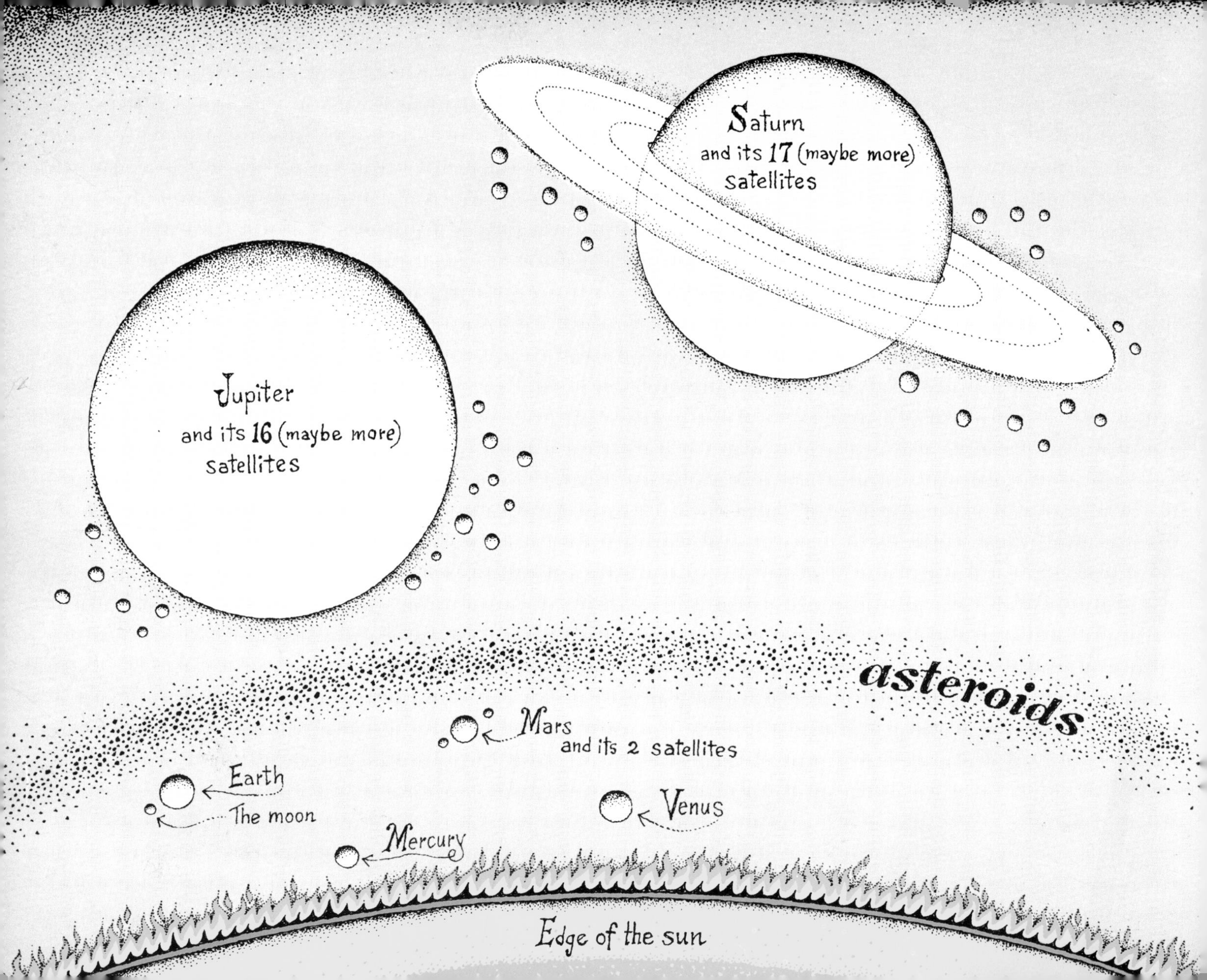

Saturn
and its 17 (maybe more)
satellites

Jupiter
and its 16 (maybe more)
satellites

asteroids

Mars
and its 2 satellites

Earth
The moon

Venus

Mercury

Edge of the sun

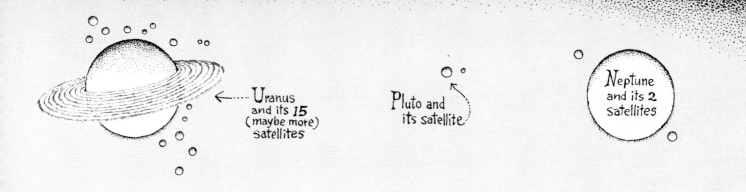

Uranus
and its 15
(maybe more)
satellites

Pluto and
its satellite

Neptune
and its 2
satellites

   The solar system has many parts—the sun, the
nine planets, the satellites of the planets, asteroids,
comets, and meteoroids. But the main parts are
the sun and the nine planets.

15

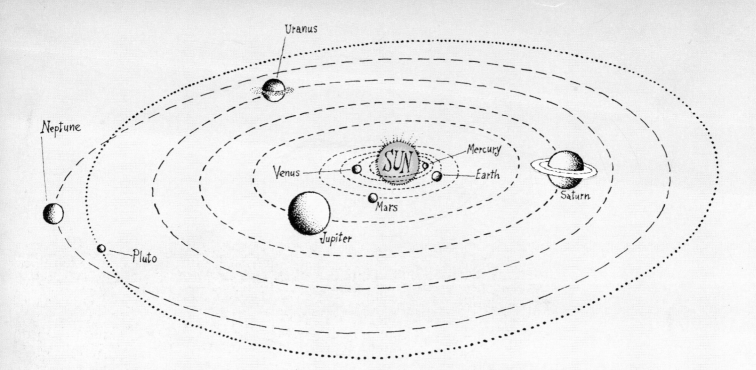

The nine planets move around the sun. They
move in paths called orbits. The drawing shows
where the orbits are, but you can't really see orbits
in space.

Mercury takes only 88 days to go around the sun once.

Pluto takes much longer than that. It takes about 248 years!

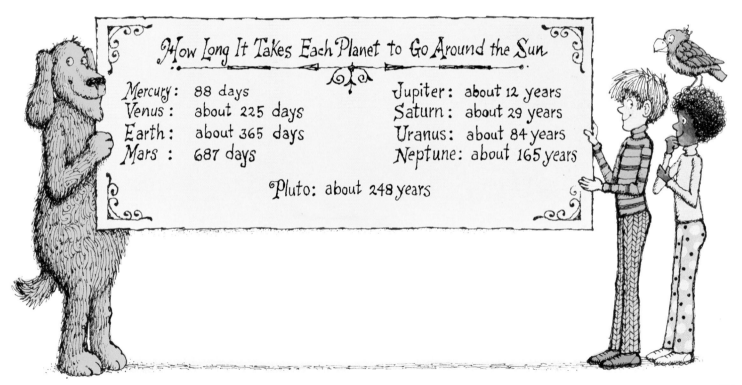

How Long It Takes Each Planet to Go Around the Sun

Mercury: 88 days
Venus: about 225 days
Earth: about 365 days
Mars: 687 days

Jupiter: about 12 years
Saturn: about 29 years
Uranus: about 84 years
Neptune: about 165 years

Pluto: about 248 years

Mercury is closer to the sun than any other planet, but even Mercury is millions of miles away from the sun.

Suppose you could fly from Mercury to the sun in a rocket. And suppose the rocket went 50,000 miles an hour. It would take more than four weeks to get there.

It would take over eight years for the rocket to get from Neptune to the sun.

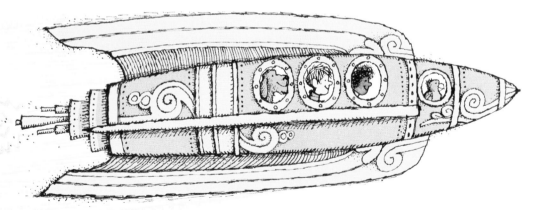

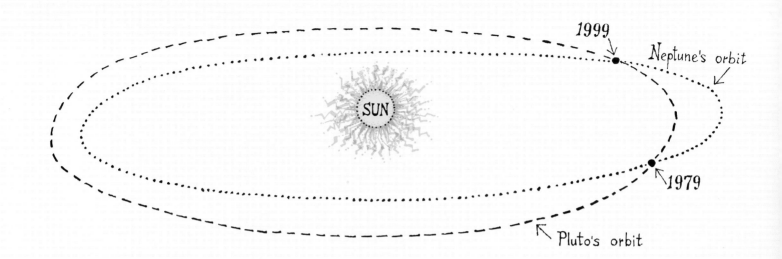

Neptune is farther from the sun than any other planet, but it wasn't always. Pluto was the farthest planet. Then, in 1979, for the first time in hundreds of years, Pluto was a little closer to the sun than Neptune.

In 1999, Pluto will again become the farthest planet from the sun. How old will you be in 1999?

The planets get most of their heat from the sun, which is very, very hot.

The sun

Temperature on the surface of the sun: about 11,000°F

Temperature at the center of the sun: about 25,000,000°F

Both Neptune and Pluto are far away from the sun. That is why they are the coldest planets. Temperatures on these planets are about 328 degrees below zero Fahrenheit.

That's much colder than any place on Earth. Even the South Pole never gets that cold.

Mercury and Venus are the hottest planets. The temperature on Mercury reaches 600 degrees Fahrenheit. On Venus it reaches 860 degrees Fahrenheit.

Plants and animals cannot live on Mercury or Venus. They would burn up. They cannot live on Neptune or Pluto either. They would freeze.

Of all the planets, Earth is the only one on which people live. In fact, we think no other planet in our solar system has plants or animals of any kind. Earth is the "life planet."

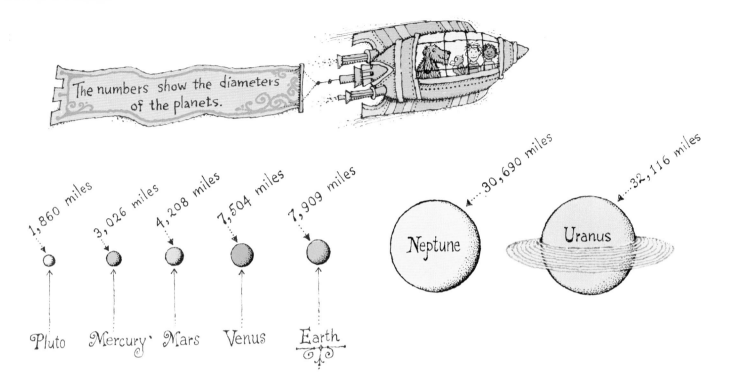

The numbers show the diameters of the planets.

1,860 miles — Pluto

3,026 miles — Mercury

4,208 miles — Mars

7,504 miles — Venus

7,909 miles — Earth

30,690 miles — Neptune

32,116 miles — Uranus

Earth is a middle-sized planet. Four of the planets are smaller than Earth. They are Mercury, Venus, Mars, and Pluto. Four of the planets are larger than Earth. They are Jupiter, Saturn, Uranus, and Neptune.

Jupiter is the biggest of all the planets.

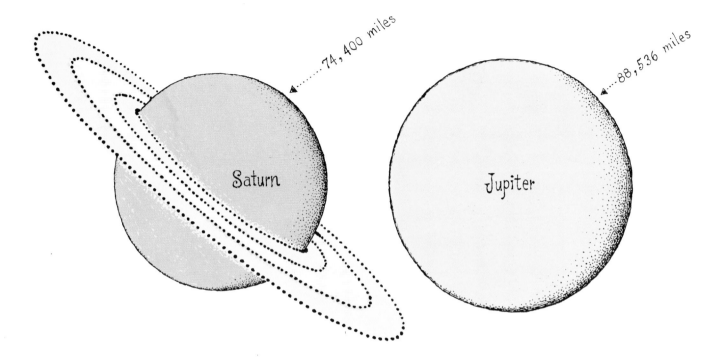

It is much bigger than Earth. Suppose Jupiter
were a large, hollow ball. Over 1,000 Earths
could fit inside it.

Pluto is the smallest planet. It is much smaller
than Earth. More than 100,000 Plutos would fit
inside Jupiter.

You can make a mobile of the solar system that will show the differences in the sizes of the planets.

Copy the circles on these two pages. Then cut them out of cardboard. Jupiter and Saturn will be very big.

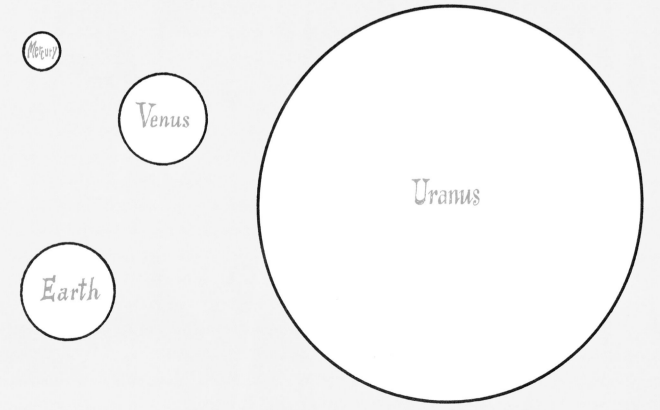

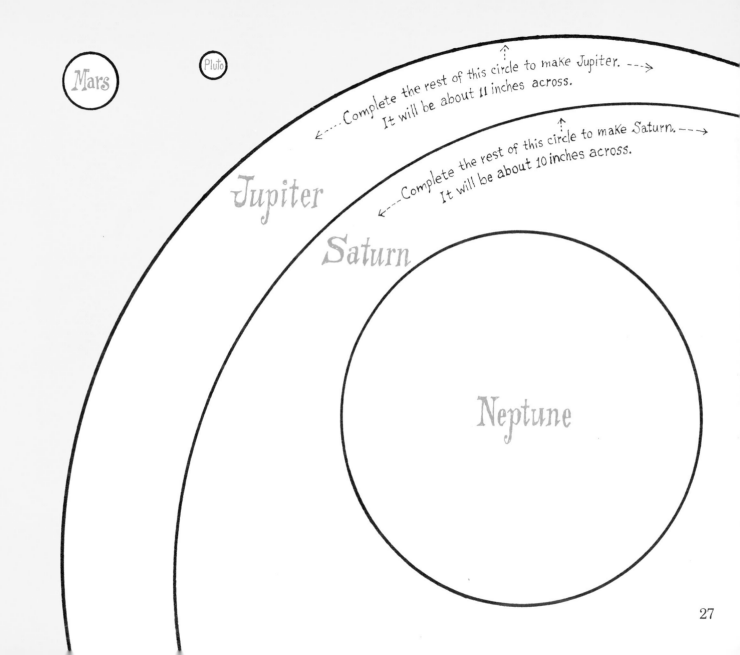

Mars

Pluto

←----Complete the rest of this circle to make Jupiter. ---→
It will be about 11 inches across.

Jupiter

←---Complete the rest of this circle to make Saturn. --→
It will be about 10 inches across.

Saturn

Neptune

1. After you have cut out the circles, tape or glue pieces of thread or light string to them. Make each string about four inches long.

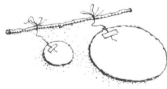

2. Gather five small twigs. They don't have to be the same length.

3. Tie the string from Jupiter to one end of a twig. Tie another planet—any one of them—to the other end of the twig. You can tape the strings in place if you want to.

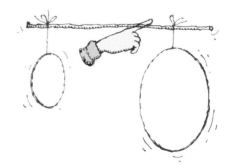

4. Lay the twig across your finger. Move the twig from side to side until it balances. Mark that place. This is the balance point.

5. Tie a string around the mark. The planets should balance. If they don't, move the string along the twig until they do. Tape the string in place.

6. Fasten the other planets to twigs. Balance the twigs on your finger. Tie strings around the balance points.

7. One of the twigs will have only one planet, but that's all right. If the planet is a little one, the stick will still balance on your finger.

8. Tie the string from each twig to the balance point of another twig. All the twigs together make a mobile. Hurrah!

Hurrah!

9. If your mobile does not balance evenly, try moving the strings a little. Or you can hang small cardboard strips on the twigs. They add weight.

Here is another model you can make. This one shows the nine planets and their distances from the sun. To make this model, you'll need a long wall.

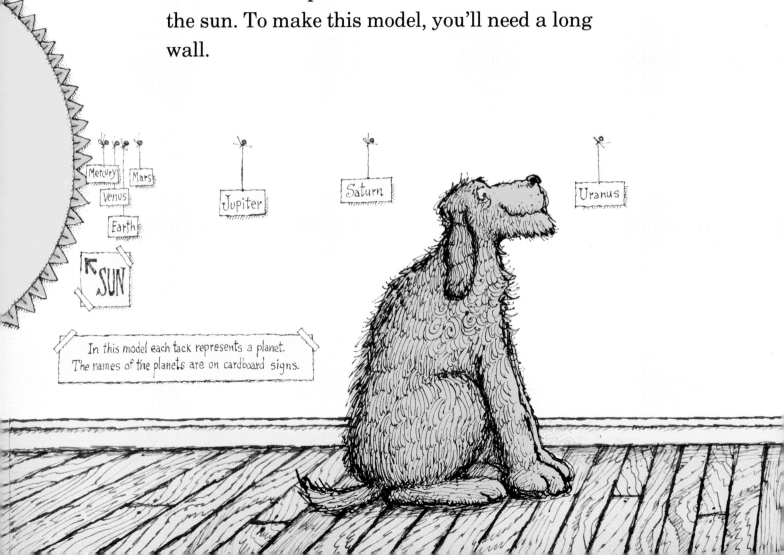

In this model each tack represents a planet. The names of the planets are on cardboard signs.

Write the names of the planets on pieces of cardboard. The drawing shows how far from the sun each of the planets should be. Pick a point on the wall to be the sun. Measure, then put the cardboard signs where they belong.

Earth is the most important planet to you, and to all of us. That's because it's the planet on which we live. It is not the biggest planet in the solar system, nor is it the smallest. It is not the hottest, nor the coldest. Earth is about in the middle. And it's just right for us.

HOORAY FOR THE PLANET EARTH!